Cornerstones of Freedom

African-Americans in the Thirteen Colonies

Deborah Kent

CHILDREN'S PRESS®
A Division of Grolier Publishing
New York • London • Hong Kong • Sydney
Danbury, Connecticut

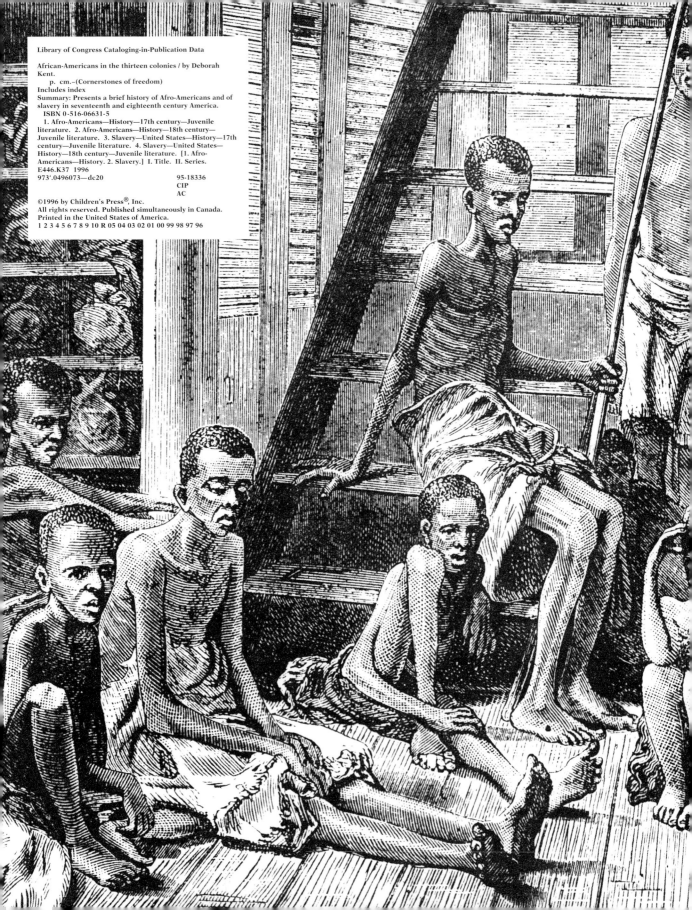

Library of Congress Cataloging-in-Publication Data

African-Americans in the thirteen colonies / by Deborah Kent.
    p. cm.–(Cornerstones of freedom)
Includes index
Summary: Presents a brief history of Afro-Americans and of slavery in seventeenth and eighteenth century America.
    ISBN 0-516-06631-5
    1. Afro-Americans—History—17th century—Juvenile literature. 2. Afro-Americans—History—18th century—Juvenile literature. 3. Slavery—United States—History—17th century—Juvenile literature. 4. Slavery—United States—History—18th century—Juvenile literature. [1. Afro-Americans—History. 2. Slavery.] I. Title. II. Series.
E446.K37 1996
973'.0496073—dc20   95-18336
                                     CIP
                                     AC

In 1619, the English colonist John Rolfe wrote in his journal: "About the last of August came in a Dutch man of warre that sold us twenty negars." Rolfe owned a tobacco farm in Jamestown, a settlement in the Virginia Colony. His brief sentence described the first time that people from Africa were imported into the English-controlled colonies of North America to serve as slaves. The twenty Africans who left the ship were the first of a great wave of men and women who would come to the colonies in chains.

An early group of African slaves arrives in Jamestown.

The explorer Balboa had a crew made up of black and white men when he reached the Pacific Ocean in 1513.

The slaves who were brought to Jamestown were not the first people of African origin to come to the New World. At least one African served with Christopher Columbus when he crossed the Atlantic Ocean in 1492. Some twenty years later, black people were part of Balboa's crew as he crossed the Isthmus of Panama and reached the Pacific Ocean. Africans marched with Cortés during the exploration of Mexico. The black trailblazer Estéban acted as a guide during the earliest European expeditions into what is now the southern United States.

Year after year, ships brought more slaves from Africa to the Virginia Colony. The first slaves worked side by side in the fields with white indentured servants. An indentured servant was a European man or woman who

For centuries, African-Americans endured heavy labor in plantation fields, either as slaves or as indentured servants.

was given passage to America by a farm owner in the colonies. In return for the voyage, the indentured servant had to work for the farmer, usually for four to seven years.

At first, farmers in Virginia treated the Africans the same way they treated their white indentured servants. They gave the servants their freedom after a period of bondage. The issue of race seemed unimportant. Landowners referred to anyone in the indentured class as a "servant," without mentioning the person's skin color. Black and white servants often became close friends. The whites taught the Africans the English language. In turn, the blacks entertained the English with their folktales and dances and shared their arts and handicrafts. Africans and Europeans intermarried freely. These interracial couples' children were fully accepted into society.

This period of racial equality in the colonies lasted for about forty years. Black people who gained their freedom could vote, hold public office, and serve in the militia. Some became prominent figures. Anthony Johnson arrived as a slave, but he became a respected Virginia landowner. In the neighboring Maryland Colony, Mathias Sousa worked off his servitude and then grew rich by trading with the Native Americans. Eventually, Sousa was elected to the Maryland Assembly.

Despite this promising beginning, the greed of the colonists eventually doomed the Africans to bondage. As trade with England expanded, crops such as indigo, tobacco, and rice became increasingly profitable. These crops could be grown most efficiently on plantations that employed large labor crews. For a time, plantation owners considered enslaving Native Americans. But the Indians knew the terrain well and could escape easily. Indentured servants worked hard, but when they achieved their freedom, they quickly left the plantations. Farm owners used black slaves because they were relatively inexpensive, and the supply of Africans seemed endless. Unlike English servants, the Africans could not appeal to their government if a master broke the terms of a labor contract. Africans who were forced to toil in the fields for life proved to be the cheapest available workforce.

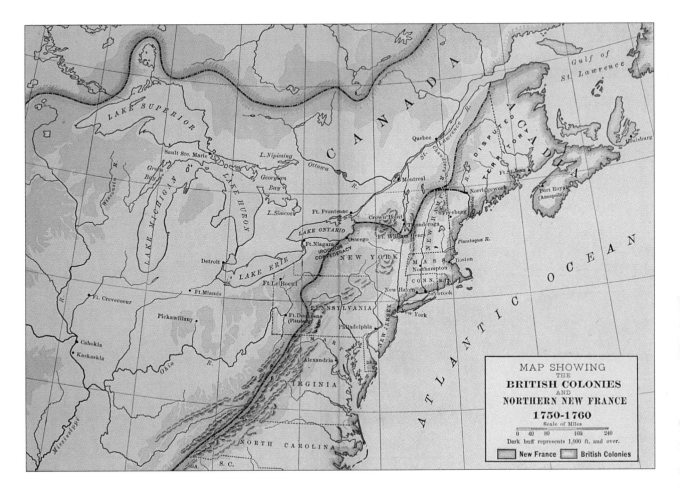

Map showing the British Colonies and Northern New France 1750-1760.

This map dated 1750 shows the eastern portion of North America, including the thirteen British colonies and Canadian territories controlled by France. The British Colonial Era would soon end with the Revolutionary War and the establishment of the United States of America in 1776.

Throughout the 1600s, African-American slaves had been kept in all thirteen British colonies. But by the end of the Revolutionary War, several northern states had outlawed slavery. Slavery was legal only in the South until the end of the Civil War in 1865.

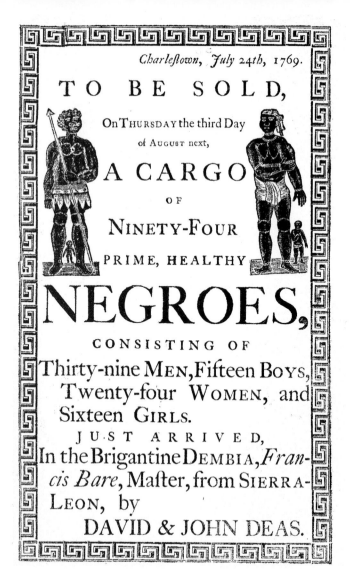

Charlestown, July 24th, 1769.

TO BE SOLD,

On Thursday the third Day of August next,

A CARGO

OF

NINETY-FOUR

PRIME, HEALTHY

NEGROES,

CONSISTING OF

Thirty-nine MEN, Fifteen BOYS, Twenty-four WOMEN, and Sixteen GIRLS.

JUST ARRIVED,

In the Brigantine DEMBIA, *Francis Bare*, Master, from SIERRA-LEON, by

DAVID & JOHN DEAS.

During the 1600s, Virginia and Maryland passed laws rescinding the custom of giving black indentured servants their freedom. Under the new laws, slavery became a lifelong condition. Marriage between blacks and whites became strictly forbidden. Babies born to a slave woman became the property of her master. Blacks were looked upon as chattel—possessions to be bought and sold without emotion.

Upon arrival in the colonies, African slaves endured the humiliation of being auctioned as if they were animals or objects.

By the mid-1700s, thirteen British colonies stretched along the Atlantic coast. A census taken in 1740 counted 150,024 slaves in the colonies. The vast majority of these slaves lived in the South. In South Carolina, where rice was grown in abundance, there were actually more slaves than white people. It is ironic that rice was one of the crops that helped to make slavery profitable. Rice was cultivated widely in Africa, and black field hands in South Carolina had urged their masters to grow it. The Africans knew rice would thrive in the colony's warm, humid climate. But growing rice demands a large number of farmworkers, so plantation owners began buying more and more slaves.

As the colonies prospered, thousands of new slaves arrived each year. Most of them came

African-American slaves hoeing rice

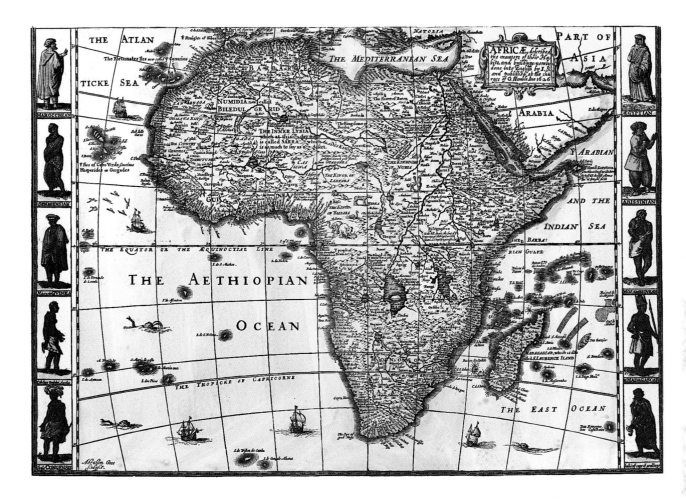

from West Africa, where they were citizens of well-established nation-states such as Dahomey, Hausa, and Ashanti. These nations had kings, court systems, and flourishing markets. American slaves came from all social classes. In Africa, they had been princes, peasants, doctors, and priests. Slavery erased all such distinctions. As American slaves, kings and paupers were equals. They were stripped of their human identities.

This map of Africa in the 1600s shows some of the many tribes that populated the continent.

In the course of history, nearly all peoples—European, Asian, African, and Native American—have practiced slavery in one form or another. In biblical times, slavery was considered a natural condition of life. Some African societies used enslavement to punish criminals or people who could not pay back their debts. Slavery was often the fate of African prisoners of war. But long-standing African customs demanded that a slave must be released after a given period of time.

This detail from an ancient Egyptian temple wall shows slaves tied together by a rope around their necks.

The rules changed, though, during the decades after Europeans arrived in America. Slaves were needed to work on the sugar plantations of the West Indies and Brazil, and to tend rice and tobacco crops in the North American colonies. Slave traders made such high profits that they referred to Africans as "black gold."

European slave traders flocked to the shores of Africa, eager to bid for human merchandise. Their demand for slaves triggered a series of wars among the African tribes. The traders promised African warlords guns, molasses, and rum in exchange for captives. Raiding parties swept into villages and carried away men, women, and children. The prisoners were marched to the coast, where they saw great sailing ships bobbing at anchor. Few could have imagined the terrible fate that lay in store for them as they were herded aboard.

Strangely, many slave ships bore glorious names: the *Gift of God,* the *Brotherhood,* the *Justice,* and even the *Liberty.* Before boarding, each captive was branded on the breast with a hot iron, leaving the mark of a particular trader. Stark naked and in chains, the prisoners were then packed together in cargo holds belowdecks. One European captain said, "They [the captives] had not so much room as a man in his coffin."

The voyage across the Atlantic Ocean lasted several months. With no bathroom facilities, the stench in the slave quarters was suffocating. Sailors at sea claimed they smelled a slave ship long before they sighted one. Diseases ran rampant in the cramped holds. At least one in ten captives died during the passage. A slave sometimes awoke to find himself chained to a corpse. So many dead were thrown overboard that schools of hungry sharks followed the ships all the way across the ocean.

White slave traders often made deals with African warriors to capture Africans of other tribes and deliver them as slaves. At right is an illustration of such an African slave hunter.

Once captured, families of innocent Africans were bound together and taken to a nearby port (left). Then, they were loaded onto overcrowded slave ships for the journey across the Atlantic Ocean (below).

Store Room.

Store Room.

This sketch is an overhead view of a ship's cramped cargo hold in which hundreds of slaves traveled to North America.

On a few occasions, revolts broke out aboard the slave ships. Sometimes, captives broke their chains and attacked the ships' crews with the severed links. Against men armed with guns, these prisoners had little chance of success. A 1721 revolt aboard the slave ship *Robert* was started by a woman captive. A white crew member wrote of the punishment imposed on her by the ship's captain: "The woman was hoisted up by her thumbs, and whipped and slashed with knives before the other slaves till she died."

Between 1500 and 1800, European traders shipped approximately ten million black people from Africa to the New World. The overwhelming majority went to the West Indies, Brazil, or other Latin American colonies. About five percent of the human cargo found its way to the thirteen British colonies in North America.

At slave auctions in the colonies, naked men and women were lined up and inspected as if they were cattle. Prospective buyers felt the

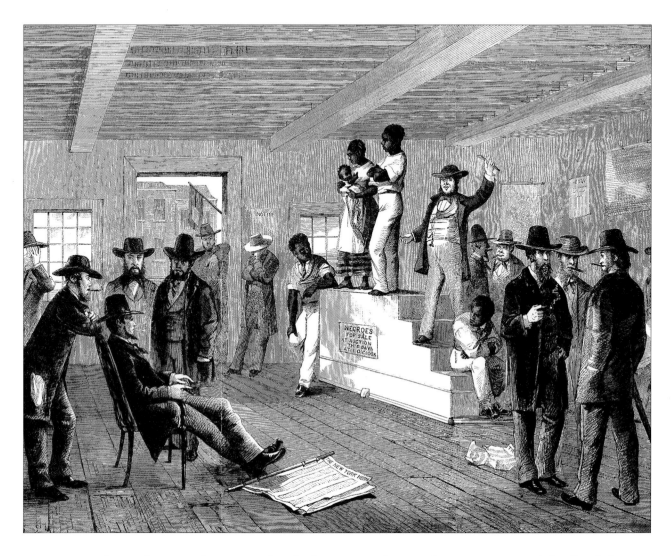

slaves' muscles, studied their teeth, and examined their skin for signs of disease. The slaves had no control over what would happen next. They might be sold to an owner who treated slaves kindly, or to a brutal master who worked them to death.

A family of slaves is auctioned. Often families were split apart forever when different owners purchased other family members.

Detail from *Alexander Spotswood Payne and His Brother, John Robert Dandridge Payne, with their Nurse*, attributed to Payne Limner, 1790–1800.

Slave nurses took care of white plantation owners' children.

The vast majority of slaves were put to work in the fields. Some drew special assignments, becoming cooks, housekeepers, bricklayers, or barrelmakers. Black women were often given the responsibility of tending white children.

It was possible for a slave to earn money and buy his or her freedom. But colonial laws discouraged this practice. Most white colonists were frightened by the thought of a large community of free black people. They feared a massive black revolt led by free men and women and fueled by the rage of the slaves.

Though the lives of slaves were rigidly controlled, uprisings sometimes did occur. One such rebellion erupted in New York City in 1712. Fighting as if they had nothing to lose, slaves and free blacks killed nine whites and burned several buildings before they were overpowered by the militia. To make an example of the rebels, colonial authorities sentenced several of them to death by burning at the stake. For decades afterward, white New Yorkers were haunted by the fear of another black uprising. Then, in 1741, a series of mysterious fires caused panic throughout the city. Black people, both slave and free, were rounded up, put on trial, and executed by hanging and burning.

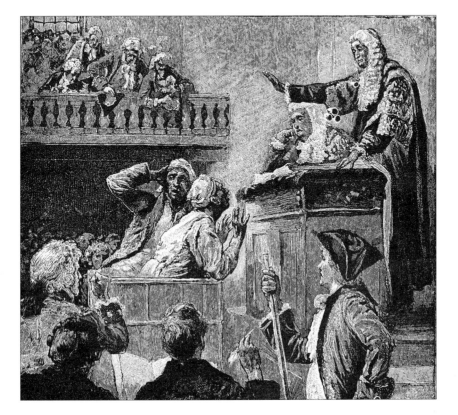

Blacks are tried in conjunction with civil unrest in New York City in 1741.

Cotton Mather

Overall, however, few slaves resorted to violence. Instead, they relied on passive resistance to make their lives bearable. A cruel master might find his farm plagued by a rash of broken plows, shovels, and pick handles. Slaves also banded together and worked very slowly to protest a master's cruelty. These work slowdowns were especially effective at harvest time, when the slaves could allow valuable crops to rot in the fields.

African-Americans in the colonies were also responsible for some truly remarkable achievements. Many black people found the courage and strength to rise above their lowly place in society and make tremendous contributions to colonial life. In 1721, a Massachusetts slave named Onesimus told his master, Cotton Mather, of a method used by African doctors to protect people during epidemics. People were intentionally given a mild dose of the infection, which prevented them from becoming dangerously ill later on. Mather, an influential clergyman, discussed the method with a colonial doctor. Their conversation led to the first smallpox inoculations given on the American continent.

The first black doctor to practice in the colonies was James Derham, who was born a slave in 1767. His master was a doctor who respected Derham's intelligence. The doctor encouraged Derham to read his medical books and to watch him and other doctors at work. Derham later became a leading physician in New Orleans.

The brilliant black scientist Benjamin Banneker was born near Baltimore in 1731. Never a slave, he attended a small school open to black and white students. As a boy, he showed a genius for science and math, and he developed an interest in astronomy. At age twenty-two he built an extraordinary clock. All of its pieces were carved from wood. Though Banneker had never seen a clock before, the instrument that he created kept perfect time for the next fifty years. Banneker is most famous as one of the surveyors who laid out the boundaries of a swampy area of Maryland where the United States built its new capital city, Washington, D.C.

Benjamin Banneker

The title page to Phillis Wheatley's book of poems, published in 1773

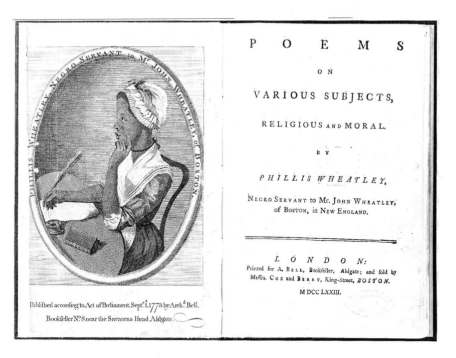

Phillis Wheatley was born in Africa in 1753. She was captured and enslaved at the age of eight. Eventually, she worked as a slave for a family in Boston. Impressed by the girl's quickness, her mistress taught her to read. Wheatley mastered the English language so thoroughly that she became an accomplished poet. One of her poems, in praise of George Washington, was read and cherished by the general, himself. Another poem lamented the system of slavery:

> *I, young in life, by seeming cruel fate*
> *Was snatch'd from Afric's fancy'd seat,*
> *Such, such my case. And can I but pray*
> *Others may never feel tyrannic sway!*

By the 1770s, men and women of African descent owned thriving businesses in every colony. Samuel Fraunces ran a popular hotel and restaurant in New York City that was visited by George Washington. A black couple, Emmanuel and Mary Bernoon, operated a restaurant in Providence, Rhode Island. It was one of the largest businesses in the town. Other blacks ran stores, owned fishing boats, and published newspapers and magazines. Jean Baptiste Pointe du Sable was a successful fur trader who ventured into the western wilderness. He was the first non-Native American to settle at the site of present-day Chicago, Illinois.

Jean Baptiste Pointe du Sable was born in St. Marc, Sainte-Domingue (now Haiti). He established a fur-trading settlement on Lake Michigan that later became the city of Chicago. He lived there for twenty years and is today considered the city's founder.

The 1770 British conflict with colonists in Boston became known as the Boston Massacre. In this fight, runaway slave Crispus Attucks was killed (right, on ground).

In the late 1760s, a new spirit of independence swept through the thirteen colonies. To pay the debts from the French and Indian War (1756–63), the king of England levied new taxes on the colonies. These measures—starting with the Stamp Act of 1765—stirred resentment among the colonists. Cautiously, the words "freedom" and "independence" were whispered from one colonial household to another.

As tensions in America mounted, England sent troops to occupy New York and Boston. On March 5, 1770, a crowd gathered in Boston and began hurling insults at some British soldiers. The British opened fire, killing three people and wounding eight others. The incident, remembered as the Boston Massacre, stirred the fires of American patriotism. One of the Bostonians to fall before the British guns was Crispus Attucks, a former slave who had run away from his master years before. Historians consider Attucks the first casualty in the American Revolution.

On July 4, 1776, the Continental Congress in Philadelphia approved the Declaration of Independence, breaking the ties between the colonies and England. Many African-Americans heard the declaration read aloud at town meetings and in village squares. They must have thrilled to the glorious words, "We hold these truths to be self-evident: that all men are created equal, that they are endowed by their Creator with certain inalienable Rights, that among these are Life, Liberty, and the pursuit of Happiness." Perhaps, they dreamed, this struggle for freedom would mean liberty for black people as well as white.

Crowds celebrate the signing of the Declaration of Independence in 1776.

A thirty-seven-year-old slave woman named Bett from Sheffield, Massachusetts, was inspired by the Declaration of Independence. After pondering the exciting new words for the next five years, she finally decided to act upon them. She visited a lawyer and explained that she wanted to sue for her freedom. She claimed that her enslavement was against the terms of the new Massachusetts Constitution. The lawyer accepted her case, and, after a trial, a jury awarded Bett her liberty. Years later, the former slave (who gave herself the new name Elizabeth Freeman) explained, "Any time while I was a slave, if one minute's freedom had been offered to me, and I had been told that I must die at the end of that minute, I would have taken it—just to stand one minute on God's earth a free woman—I would!"

Throughout the Revolutionary War (1775–83), about five thousand slaves and free blacks served with honor in local militias and in the Continental Army and Navy. Blacks stood shoulder to shoulder with whites at Lexington and Concord, the first battles of the war. Together, black and white troops repulsed the British at the famous Battle of Bunker Hill. One hero in the Bunker Hill encounter was the African-American Salem Poor, praised by his commander as a "brave and gallant soldier."

During later conflicts in American history, the military was strictly segregated according to race. But army units in the Revolution were fully integrated. White and black soldiers marched together, ate together, fought and died together. A Hessian army officer who fought for the British wrote, "No [American] regiment is seen in which there are not Negroes in abundance, and among them are able-bodied, strong and brave fellows." Yet, slaves were not even free to fight in the war unless given permission by their masters. During the conflict, thousands of slaves forged their own freedom by escaping to Spanish-controlled Florida or to the French region of Canada. Others joined the British, whose leaders tried to start a slave revolt in the colonies by offering the slaves their freedom.

In this photograph from the 1860s, slaves are carrying cotton from the fields. The U.S. Civil War was fought partly over the issue of slavery in the South.

The Revolutionary War dealt the first blows to American slavery. In 1777, the territory of Vermont prohibited slavery within its borders. By 1804, all of the northern states had passed laws aimed at eliminating slavery.

But in the South, slavery remained the law of the land. With the nation divided into free (northern) and slave (southern) states, tensions mounted through the mid-1800s. War broke out after the South decided to leave the Union in 1861 and form its own nation where slavery would be legal. The Civil War lasted from 1861 to 1865, and in the end, the North prevailed. With victory in the war, Congress ensured that slavery would never blight the land again. In 1865, it passed the Thirteenth Amendment to the Constitution, which abolished slavery in the United States.

But the legal end to slavery did not bring an end to African-Americans' suffering. Generations of "free" blacks were subject to racial discrimination, ridicule, torture, and murder. It was not until the civil rights movement of the 1950s and 1960s that African-Americans gained true power and liberty in the United States. And for many, the struggle for equal treatment continues today, nearly four centuries after the first chained and enslaved Africans landed in North America.

GLOSSARY

bondage – slavery; the state of being held or controlled against one's will

calamity – disastrous event

census – official count of population

chattel – piece of personal property

epidemic – disease that spreads to many members of a group

Hessian – paid German soldier serving in the British forces during the American Revolution

indentured servant – person who legally bound himself or herself to work for a master for a period of time

indigo – dark blue dye obtained from plants

inoculation – medical treatment (such as an injection) that prevents a disease

insurrection – revolt against a ruling organization

passive resistance – nonviolent act of defiance toward authority, such as slaves stopping work to protest an overseer's cruel treatment

rescind – to take away; remove

Stamp Act – taxes placed on the colonies by England in the 1760s